R.E.I. Editions

All of our ebooks can be read on the following devices:
- Computers
- eReaders
- iOS
- Android
- Blackberries
- Windows
- Tablet
- Cell phone

French Academy

Svadhishtana

The Second chakra

ISBN: 978-2-37297-3557

Publication: February 2019
New updated edition: January 2023
Copyright © 2019 - 2023 R.E.I. Editions
www.rei-editions.com

Work plan

1- Muladhara - The First Chakra

2 - Svadhishtana - The second Chakra

3 - Manipura - The Third Chakra

4 - Anahata - The Fourth Chakra

5 - Vishuddha - The Fifth Chakra

6 - Ajna - The Sixth Chakra

7 - Sahasrara - The Seventh Chakra

French Academy

Svadhishtana
The Second Chakra

R.E.I. Editions

Book Index

The chakra system 11

Svadhishtana - The Second Chakra 15

How to activate the 2st chakra................................... 21

Color of the second chakra... 22

Essential oils associated with the second chakra 26

    Sandalwood 27

    Jasmine 30

    Bergamot 34

    Petit Grain... 37

    Myrrh 39

    Ylang Ylang.. 42

    Neroli 46

    Hyssop... 50

    Rose... 53

Himalayan flowers for the second chakra 57

    Well Being.. 59

Californian flowers for the second chakra 61

    Basil 63

    Calla Lily 64

    Easter Lily 65

    Hibiscus 65

    Sticky Monkeyflower 67

Australian flowers for the second chakra 69

    Flannel Flower 71

    She Oak 73

Bach flowers for the second chakra 75

    Rock Rose 77

    Mimulus 79

    Cherry Plum 80

    Aspen 81

    Red Chestnut 82

    Rescue Remedy 83

    Wild Oat 85

    Century 87

    Star of Bethlehem 89

- Number of the second chakra 90
- Phisical exercises 94
- Stones for the 2st Chakra 97
  - Coral 98
  - Carnelian 100
  - Eye of the Tiger 102
  - Jade 105
  - Heliotrope 107
  - Selenite 108
  - Aragonite 110
  - Aventurine 112
  - Stone of the sun 113

The chakra system

The word Chakra, which comes from Sanskrit and means "wheel", is meant to indicate the seven basic energy centers in the human body. Chakras are centers of subtle psychic energy located along the spine. Each of these centers is connected, at the level of subtle energies, to the main ganglia of the nerves which branch off from the vertebral column. In addition, the chakras are related to the levels of consciousness, to the archetypal elements, to the phases inherent in the development of life, to the colors, which are closely linked to the chakras, because they are found outside our body, but inside the aura , or the electromagnetic field that surrounds each person, to sounds, body functions and much, much more. The Eastern doctrine that has spread knowledge of them in the Western world considers the Chakras as openings, gateways to the essence of the human body. The chakras are usually represented inside a lotus flower, with a variable number of open petals. The open petals represent the chakra in its full opening. On each petal is written one of the fifty letters of the Sanskrit alphabet, which are considered sacred letters, therefore, divine expression. Furthermore, each of them expresses a different activity of the human being, a different state, both manifest and still potential. Each chakra resonates on a different frequency which corresponds to the colors of the rainbow.

The seven main Chakras also correspond to the seven main glands of our endocrine system. Their main function is to absorb the Universal Energy, metabolize it, break it down and convey it along the energy channels up to the nervous system, feed the auras and release energy outside. Most everyone sees them as funnels, simultaneously swirling and flowing energy back and forth. Each of the seven centers has both an anterior (usually dominant) component and a posterior (usually less dominant) component, which are intimately connected, with the exception, however, of the first and seventh, which, however, are single.

From the second to the fifth, the anterior aspect relates to feelings and emotions, while the posterior aspect relates to the will. As regards the anterior and posterior sixth, and the seventh, the correlation is with the mind and reason. The first and seventh. they also have the very important connection function for the human being: being the most external Chakras of the energy channel, they have the characteristic of placing man in relation with the Universe on one side and with the Earth on the other. The perfect functioning of the energy system is synonymous with good health. There are many techniques to open the Chakras, including Reiki, which stands out for its peculiar sweetness and for the possibility of harmonizing any energy imbalances.

Each center oversees certain organs, and has particular functions on an emotional, psychic and spiritual level. Among the seven fundamental ones, there are precise affinities.

- The First with the Seventh: Basic Energy with Spirit Energy.
- The Second with the Sixth: Energy of feeling on a material level with Energy of feeling on an extrasensory level.
- The Third with the Fifth: Energy of the working mind and personal power with Energy of the higher mind and communication.
- The Fourth: bridge between the upper three and the lower three and alchemical forge of transformation.

Each Chakra is associated with a color, which corresponds to and derives from the frequency and vibration of the center itself. Furthermore, each Chakra corresponds to a mantra, the sound of a musical note and, in some cases, even a natural element, a planet or a zodiac sign. Because the chakra system is the primary processing center for every function of our being, blockage or energetic insufficiency in the chakras usually causes unrest in body, mind, or spirit. A defect in the flow of energy through a given chakra will cause a defect in the energy supplied to the connected parts of the physical body, as well as affect all levels of being. This is because an energy field is a Holistic entity; every part of it affects every other part. Essential oils are able to tune into specific chakras: their scent and their vibration gently put us in deep contact with our energy centers.

The massage with specific essential oils on the points corresponding to the chakras activates and balances their action, harmonizing and strengthening the entire body. Starting from the bottom they are:

- 1st = Muladhara
- 2nd = Swadhisthana
- 3rd = Manipura
- 4th = Anahata
- 5th = Vhishuddhi
- 6th = Ajna
- 7th = Sahasrara

Furthermore, each of the seven chakras comes to represent an important area of human psychic health, which we can briefly summarize as:

1. Survival
2. Sexuality
3. Strength
4. Love
5. Communication
6. Intuition
7. Cognition.

Metaphorically the chakras are related to the following archetypal elements:

1. Earth
2. Water
3. Fire
4. Air
5. Sound
6. Light
7. Thought

Svadhishtana - The Second Chakra

The second chakra is called the "sacral chakra", the center of the cross.
Its symbol is the orange lotus with six petals; the letters Bam, Bham, Mam, Yam, Ram and Lam of the Sanskrit alphabet are inscribed on these petals. It is located in the lower abdomen, just above the pubis, in correspondence with the sacrum (three fingers below the navel near the sacral plexus). The second is the chakra of the continuation of the species and, therefore, of reproduction and as a logical consequence it is the source of energy and sexual pleasure. Its symbol is the upward-facing crescent moon. The key word is "I feel", the bodily feeling of sensations, whether pleasant or unpleasant. It develops from about the seventh year of age until about the fourteenth. In women it turns clockwise, in men counterclockwise. The second chakra is associated with the emotional body, the water element, taste (tongue) and action (hands). The glands controlled by it are the gonads (ovaries and testicles).

Its function is linked to desire, pleasure, sexuality, procreation, the ability to experience non-mental primordial emotions. The organs connected with the second Chakra are: intestine, bladder, uterus, ovaries, prostate. The kidneys are just the symbol of fear. The dysfunctions of the second Chakra cause impotence, frigidity, pathologies of the genital system, also at the lesion level (fibromas, prostate adenomas), of the urinary system and lumbosacral stiffness. From a psychological point of view, a decompensated second Chakra leads to lack of self-esteem, phobias, panic and anxiety. From an emotional point of view, the imbalance of this Chakra can lead to the obsessive search for pleasure, also and above all on a sexual level up to aberration, if it is hyperfunctioning, but also to a total closure towards the sexuality of life, generating a sort of anesthesia of the ability to experience non-intellectual joy, if it is instead hypofunctional..

This Chakra is often found decompensated in female subjects (it should be remembered that the proper polarity of this Chakra, like that of all even Chakras, is Yin).

The second Chakra indicates our emotional part, our fears, the things that have scared us, that paralyze us. It is the first step of energy towards dematerialization. It

is always worth remembering that the four alchemical principles are basically the four principles of energy:
- 1st principle: in one is all, that is, in my cell the same thing happens that happens in the cell of the galaxy.
- 2nd principle: matter is the invisible part of the invisible, i.e. what we see materialized, is the part that we have made tangible with respect to the homologous invisible energy.
- 3rd principle: as above so below and vice versa, i.e. Yin and Yang, black and white, day and night, light and dark, i.e. what happens on one level also happens on the other other level.
- 4th principle: nature is constantly renewed by fire, which means that only in faith what burns inside you allows you to renew your life.

By acting on the second chakra, what is commonly referred to as the self-healing process is achieved. Once balanced, its positive energy will expand to all other chakras accordingly. It is therefore a very important chakra (as indeed are the others), whose correct activity allows the human being to appreciate life and, therefore, make it easier and more pleasant in a certain sense, and not only with the half of the sky, or on the contrary, in the event of an incorrect flow, transform it into a small but very efficient personal hell which ends up also reflecting on those who are nearby: wife, husband, partner, children, parents.

This subtle center gravitates around the Nabhi, like a satellite, thus delimiting the region of the Void. It is the only mobile chakra.

It is described as a very energetic centre, especially in men who would emit a large amount of energy with the sperm during orgasm (in China ejaculation is also called "little death").

The deity in charge is Varuna, her vital energy or Shakti is Sarasvati. It is located inside the sushumna at the base of the genital organ.

The related element is water, represented by a white circular mandala in which a crescent moon inscribed between two lotus flowers stands out.

The main feature of this chakra is fluidity and the concentration operated on svadhishthana favors the refreshing action. The bijamantra is «vam», i.e. the letter «va» nasalized, that is pronounced making it resonate in the nose. It is the bijamantra of the god Varuna, lord of the sky in the most ancient period of Hindu civilization, the one centered on the sacred collections of the Vedas, and therefore god of the ocean in more recent times. The bijamantra is visualized as a deity holding a white lace in her hand on the makara, a mythical sea monster, mount of Varuna and of the goddess Ganga, the river Ganges. In the dot that is placed on the letter of the Sanskrit alphabet to nasalize it, another divinity is inscribed, Hari, or the god Vishnu, lord of the preservation of life, represented here as a blue-skinned adolescent with a yellow-gold robe, endowed with four arms in whose hands are the club, the conch, the sharp disc and the lotus, with a curl of hair on the chest symbolizing nature and a gem on the heart symbolizing souls. His mount is Garuda, the vulture with human features.

Shakti, the feminine cosmic energy, is projected here as Rakini, terrifying goddess on a red lotus, in a furious aspect, as underlined by the evident fangs, and drunk with ambrosia, with a blue complexion, with three eyes and four arms in the whose hands are a spear, a lotus, a tambourine, and a sharp axe. She is fond of rice and is associated with blood, one of the seven components traditional Indian medicine believes make up the body.

The geometric figures are further specified in their meaning by other symbols: the element of svadhishthana is water, depicted as nocturnal water illuminated by a quarter moon and animated by a composite mythical being in which there are also fish and crocodile.

Water, as we have already seen, is in all myths «the primordial womb of life» that can generate (or destroy) everything. So nocturnal, from a psychological point of view, it is a symbol of an unconscious and terrifying feminine that threatens to prevail or still prevails over conscious development. The moon is also a widespread symbol of the feminine in its nocturnal, dark, and therefore psychologically speaking, unconscious meaning.

Finally the "beast", half fish and half crocodile, while on the one hand it suggests a passage from water to air and therefore a development towards a higher evolutionary stage, on the other in the crocodile, confirms the dangerous and terrifying nature of the power held in the chakra.

The color of this chakra is orange.

It is possible to note that the germinative processes take place in a darkness barely illuminated by a small fire. There is therefore more heat here than in the previous chakra, because life needs a little "fire", but there is less than in the following chakra because too much fire "burns". In fact, the development of life needs tepid humidity.

How to activate the 2st chakra

- Get in touch with the water element, go swimming regularly and take pleasant hot baths in peace.
- Wear orange clothing or decorate your apartment with orange fabrics and colors.
- Drink enough, at least two liters of liquid a day in the form of water and herbal tea.
- Walk along the beach, along a river or stream, go to the lake.
- Contemplate the moonlight on full moon nights. Touch the water, bathe in the clear waters, linger on the banks of a stream, drink directly from the source of a stream and follow the water games among the stones.
- The vowel "O" stimulates the energy of the chakra; sit upright and inhale through your nose, making a closed "O" sound as you exhale. Perform the exercise for about 5 minutes a day.
- Listen to oriental music or the "fluid" music of Bach and Vivaldi.
- Lighting incense with harmonic vibrations of the second chakra.
- Use crystal therapy with stones suitable for the second chakra.

Color of the second chakra

Orange is the color of the second chakra.
Orange is a secondary color which has the strength of red tempered by the light of yellow. In oriental culture, the color orange is associated with properties that favor mental concentration. For this reason, Buddhist monks wear a habit of this color, which has the purpose of facilitating the detachment from earthly and carnal passions. It is universally traced back to the idea of the Sun, and therefore, of life, procreation and happiness. It is therefore often called "The Ray of Salvation". Unlike red, Orange "warms without burning". It is the color that mainly stimulates the endocrine action having a balancing action even in psychosomatic dysfunctions. It is no longer a color associated with opposing temperaments, those of passion, love or hate, but it is comparable to the warm, welcoming and reassuring light of the hearth, so much so that, in environments lit with this colour, people are able to communicate better and more intimately. Orange has the fundamental characteristics to help get out of the emotional state of fear because it contains red which infuses strength and courage and yellow which "illuminates" ideas and stimulates the rational mind. He manages to unite the rational (yellow) with the impulsive (red). Fear paralyzes while uncertainty and doubts uselessly burn our energies leading us away from the real goals of our lives; therefore, even if these feelings somehow hold us

back, imprison us, a warm color helps movement and therefore gives the right fuel and energy to get out of that emotion. The characteristics balanced in orange are: graceful movements, emotional intelligence (right side of the brain), knowing how to experience pleasure, knowing how to take care of oneself and others, ability to change. The choice of orange indicates the need to search for intense experiences, in every aspect, from which to draw and experience new pleasant and cognitive sensations. Red is physical strength-love and yellow wisdom-knowledge; united in orange they express this combination of characteristics. On the psyche it induces serenity, enthusiasm, joy, desire to live, increases optimism.

From a psychological point of view, a decompensated second Chakra leads to lack of self-esteem, phobias, panic and anxiety. From an emotional point of view, the imbalance of this Chakra can lead to the obsessive search for pleasure, also and above all on a sexual level up to aberration, if it is hyperfunctioning, but also to a total closure towards the sexuality of life, generating a sort of anesthesia of the ability to experience non-intellectual joy, if it is instead hypofunctional. This Chakra is often found decompensated in female subjects (it should be remembered that the proper polarity of this Chakra, like that of all even Chakras, is Yin). The second Chakra indicates our emotional part, our fears, the things that have scared us, that paralyze us. It is the first step of energy towards dematerialization. It is always worth remembering that the four alchemical principles are basically the four principles of energy:

- 1st principle: in one is all, that is, in my cell the same thing happens that happens in the cell of the galaxy.

- 2nd principle: matter is the invisible part of the invisible, i.e. what we see materialized, is the part that we have made tangible with respect to the homologous invisible energy.

- 3rd principle: as above so below and vice versa, i.e. Yin and Yang, black and white, day and night, light and dark, i.e. what happens on one level also happens on the other other level.

- 4th principle: nature is constantly renewed by fire, which means that only in faith what burns inside you allows you to renew your life.

By acting on the second chakra, what is commonly referred to as a self-healing process occurs. Once balanced, its positive energy will expand to all other chakras accordingly. It is therefore a very important chakra (as indeed are the others), whose correct activity allows the human being to appreciate life and, therefore, make it in a certain sense easier and very pleasant - and not only with the half of the sky – or on the contrary, in case of incorrect flow, transform it into a small but very efficient personal hell which ends up reflecting also on those who are nearby: wife, husband, partner, children, parents.

Remember that the electromagnetic energy of orange is on the same vibrational frequency as the DNA chain. The orange color helps eliminate shocks and blockages in the genital system, helps close the holes that form in the left side of the Aura.

The presence of this color is able to modify the anxious person on a psychological level because its action reverberates on the emotions that are the basis of affective disorders, from which all the disturbances that arise in the sphere of anxiety, generic or phobic, originate , or associated with panic attacks, compulsions and obsessions.

Essential oils associated with the second chakra

Sandalwood, jasmine, bergamot, petit grain, myrrh, ylang ylang, neroli, geranium, hyssop and rose activate the second chakra.
Mix each individual essential oil with a carrier oil, such as jojoba or almond oil, in the ratio of 2 drops per tablespoon of carrier oil, then 2 drops per 10 mL of carrier. Since this is a "vibrational treatment", a very diluted mixture will have a deeper and more marked action. Massage the chakra you want to work on with the blend containing the chosen essential oil. Use a few drops and apply them slowly with your fingertips and in a clockwise circular motion. While massaging the Chakra, focus on the result you want to achieve, visualizing the harmonic energy of the oil as it opens and rebalances the chakra. After the treatment, lie down and relax for a while, allowing the Chakra to rebalance itself. Breathe deeply and slowly, trying to clear and empty your mind as much as possible.
As an alternative to the massage, add a few drops of the essential oil chosen for the treatment to the essence diffuser. Concentrate and focus on your therapeutic intention, visualize the aromatherapy energy of the essential oil, open and rebalance the chakra. Relax for at least half an hour.

Sandalwood

For 4,000 years the aroma of sandalwood essential oil has been appreciated, so much so that it is traditionally used in Tantric Yoga schools to help awaken Kundalini, sexual energy. One of the properties of sandalwood oil is that it improves over time, i.e. it matures particular notes that make it even more pleasant. Unfortunately, the inconsiderate use of these trees for the vast production of oils both for curative purposes and for the production of soaps and perfumes, has caused a drastic decrease in the number of specimens which are now monitored to prevent their disappearance. On a physical level, sandalwood is one of the most delicate essential oils for the skin: it does not irritate, restores the right hydration and heals small wounds. Due to its antiseptic and decongestant properties it is a panacea for respiratory tract problems.

1. Part used - wood and roots.
2. Extraction method - steam distillation.
3. Base note: woody, sweet, balsamic, intense scent.

- **Aphrodisiac**

Transform sexual energy by elevating it to the spiritual plane. It reduces aggression and violent instincts, loosens exasperation and releases blocked sexual energy. Sexual disorders related to depressive states are often resolved thanks to the use of this oil. It is, however, more suitable for active people than for phlegmatic subjects. Although it has always been considered a powerful and precise signal of male eros, sandalwood essential oil gives off a soft and warm force that envelops men and women with equal beneficial effects. It works by balancing sexuality with the spirit, promoting the integration of the sacred with the profane: for this reason it is used in tantra yoga schools to transform sexual energies into spiritual energies. It is therefore not a direct aphrodisiac, as its action is predominantly meditative and directed towards the interiority: it is indicated for subjects who experience sexuality in a superficial way.

- **Harmonizing**

Sandalwood essential oil balances the entire chakra energy system by calming and facilitating spiritual development. Its particular value consists in the fact that it manages to calm the mental work that often distracts those who meditate. By stilling the rational part of the mind, it allows it to enter the deeper stages of meditation. This is advisable when preparing to take a healing session and in self-healing. Transmits openness of mind, warmth and understanding. Reduces stress, calms aggression, agitation and fear, indicated in case of insomnia. It supports those who practice yoga against anxiety and depression, to find serenity.

- **Relaxing bath**

10 drops of essential oil in bath water give a pleasant feeling of relaxation. Remain immersed for at least 15 minutes. Some parents greatly appreciate the scent of sandalwood essential oil diluted in a base oil or in the bathtub in case of problems with hyperactive, stubborn children or to calm rebellious teenagers.

- **Shower**

Put 3-4 drops on a wet sponge glove and gently massage the whole body.

- **Contraindications**

Sandalwood essential oil is non-irritating, non-sensitizing and non-toxic. It is good to pay attention not to use it in case of severe kidney disease and for periods not exceeding 6 weeks. Contraindicated in pregnancy and breastfeeding. Particular caution is required at the time of purchase as it is often "cut" with lower quality essences, such as, for example, the essential oil of Australian sandalwood.

Jasmine

It is considered one of the most precious and delicate oils, on a par with rose essential oil, and certainly also among the most expensive, due to the fact that about 8,000 flowers are needed to obtain 1 liter of jasmine essential oil.

Considered by the Arabs to be the king of flowers, jasmine is mentioned, together with the rose, as a flower of love and affection, a symbol of the feminine par excellence.

A legend tells that jasmines are stars fallen to earth; they release their maximum perfume at night and are therefore linked to the two nocturnal "planets" par excellence, the Moon and Venus. These stars govern the balance of the female organism in its two psycho-emotional and reproductive aspects. For this double power, it should not be missing from those who want to experience complete harmony between mind and body.

It made its appearance in our country in the fifteenth century, brought by the Turks; instead, it arrived in the rest of the European continent in the 16th century thanks to the famous Portuguese navigator Vasco de Gama who brought home some species found in the East Indies. However, the great diffusion of jasmine dates back to the seventeenth century.

In popular medicine, it is said that the power of jasmine is such as to eradicate envy and jealousy in the people who suffer from it; again, according to tradition, jasmine would help to assume one's responsibilities and to become aware of how one acts and behaves. The maceration of the flowers in the oil is excellent if rubbed against pain from nervous inflammation.

- Part used - flowers or solvent extraction.
- Method of extraction - enfleurage or solvent extraction.
- Heart note, very intense, floral and sensual perfume.

- **Aphrodisiac**

If inhaled, it stimulates the erotic imagination and helps revive sensuality, emotions, love and compassion. For this reason it is indicated for frigidity and low libido. On a psychic level, it stimulates dedication to love and allows you to process repressed feelings, restoring peace and serenity. Relieves anxiety of sexual origin, dissolving fears in those with emotional difficulties and blocks inherent in the sphere of sexuality. It makes us appreciate beauty.

Euphorizing: if inhaled it strengthens the character, stimulates the will, and enhances self-esteem, making it more balanced and serene. Jasmine essential oil is indicated in cases of anguish and psychic crises and depression, as it overcomes pessimism, helping to overcome inertia and apathy. In fact, it seems that jasmine is able to induce optimism and euphoria, as it stimulates endorphins to lift the mood, relax the nerves, giving confidence and happiness.

Its aroma exerts a real antidepressant effect by stimulating the release of molecules such as serotonin, which promotes a good mood.

- **Rebalancing**

Massaged on the lumbar and abdominal area, starting one week before the cycle, it stimulates too scanty menstruation, facilitating blood flow in the area; counteracts the annoyances of premenstrual syndrome (bad mood, tension, headache) and, during the cycle, relieves uterine spasms, dissolving tension in the pelvic area. For this muscle relaxant action it is also effectively used to facilitate childbirth.

- **Relaxing bath**

10 drops in a tub of water has a harmonizing action, to relieve nervous tension, irritability, pre-menstrual syndrome, and allows you to work out repressed feelings. The benefits on the skin can be increased by associating jasmine with lavender and sandalwood, and a spoonful of sweet almond oil. For a luxurious aphrodisiac bath: 2 drops of jasmine essence with 3 drops of sandalwood essence and 2 drops of rose essence diluted in a spoonful of cream.

- **Contraindications**

Jasmine essential oil when used externally is non-toxic, does not irritate and does not cause sensitization. Given its concentration, it is advisable not to take it internally, as there may be toxic residues due to the solvents used for the extraction.

Bergamot

Some legends see it as originating in the Canary Islands, from which it would have been imported by Christopher Columbus, other sources favor China, Greece, or the city of Berga in Spain. One of these legends tells the story of the Moor of Spain, who sold a branch, for eighteen scudi, to the Valentino lords of Reggio Calabria, who grafted it onto a bitter orange tree, in their possession in the "Santa Caterina" district. In this province the bergamot has one of its best habitats: nowhere else in the world is there a place where this citrus fruit bears fruit with the same yield and quality of essence. Bergamot is a citrus fruit that probably derives from a cross between bitter orange and sour lime, although many believe it to be a real species called Citrus bergamia Risso (of Chinese origin). Its presence in Calabria is presumable between the fourteenth and sixteenth centuries.

In 1750 the first "bergamotte grove" would have been planted around it. 90% of the total production of bergamot comes from Calabria. It is used to combat stress and to reduce states of agitation, confusion, depression and fear, restoring optimism and serenity.

If inhaled, it induces a joyful and dynamic mood, eliminating psychological blocks. It makes one capable of giving and receiving love, of radiating happiness around oneself and caring for others.

Add 8 drops to 30-40 ml of jojoba or sweet almond oil and gently massage, with circular movements, the temples or, alternatively, two drops on the handkerchief, to be inhaled as needed. As a calming agent, it acts on the nervous system by counteracting states of anxiety, it is an effective remedy in case of insomnia, because it relaxes, reconciling sleep.

- Part used - peel of the almost ripe fruit.
- Method of extraction - cold pressing.
- Top note: soft, fresh, fruity and slightly balsamic scent.

- **Antidepressant**

In aromatherapy it is used to combat stress and to reduce states of agitation, confusion, depression and fear, restoring optimism and serenity. If inhaled, it induces a joyful and dynamic mood, eliminating psychological blocks. It makes one capable of giving and receiving love, of radiating happiness around oneself and caring for others. Add 8 drops to 30-40 ml of jojoba or sweet almond oil and gently massage, with circular movements, the temples or, alternatively, two drops on the handkerchief, to be inhaled as needed.

- **Calming**

It acts on the nervous system by counteracting anxiety states, it is an effective remedy in case of insomnia, because it relaxes, reconciling sleep.

- **Contraindications**

Bergamot essential oil is highly prized and therefore easily subject to counterfeiting; it is cut with synthetic or poor quality essences. It is important that the choice falls on quality products that pay off in terms of benefits, the oil must be very pure. Bergamot essential oil must never be used pure because it is very concentrated and can be too aggressive due to the presence of terpenes. Its effectiveness is enhanced if diluted in a carrier substance, at a concentration that never exceeds 1% (about 3 or 4 drops per 100 ml). Bergamot essential oil is phototoxic, so if applied to the skin avoid sun exposure. Furocoumarins, such as bergaptene, cause skin sensitization and pigmentation following exposure to direct sunlight. Caution is therefore necessary if the oil is applied to the skin. Apart from that, Bergamot essential oil is non-toxic and non-irritating. Do not use during pregnancy, breastfeeding and in small children. Bergamot essential oil must be protected from sunlight, because bergaptene, one of its components, becomes toxic when exposed to sunlight.

Petit Grain

Three different types of essential oils are obtained from the bitter orange plant, depending on the fresh part (drug) used:

- Neroli is obtained from the flowers with the enfleurage method.
- From the peel by mechanical pressing we will obtain the essential oil of bitter orange.
- Petit grain is distilled from fresh leaves and young twigs, which was once extracted from seeds, no longer used today, and which has a sharper scent than Neroli.

Petit grain essential oil has notable relaxing effects, and a rebalancing action on the nervous system. Like the other essences extracted from the orange plant, it improves mood, but it also has positive effects on memory. Counteracts nervousness, anxiety and stress, and promotes sleep. It is recommended for calming panic attacks. It is an excellent digestive and a valid aid in case of indigestion. Excellent deodorant, has an effective antiseptic action. Its purifying effects make it very suitable for fighting acne and skin impurities.

- Part used: leaves, branches and unripe fruits.
- Extraction method: steam distillation.

- Heart note: floral, citrus scent, with a herbaceous, woody undertone.

- **Rebalancing of the nervous system**

Petit grain essential oil soothes and refreshes the mind in case of headaches. Relaxes in the presence of irritability, nervousness, tachycardia caused by anxiety, and insomnia. It has a soothing effect on the heart, drives away negative and sad thoughts, disappointment. Calms anger and panic attacks. Prepare a massage oil by adding 5 drops of petit grain to 2 tablespoons of grape seed oil.

- **Relaxing bath**

Pour 15 drops into the bath water and immerse yourself for 10 minutes to ease nervousness, irritability, stress.
For muscle pain, mix a preparation obtained by adding 5 drops of petit grain essential oil, 2 of cajeput and 3 of rosemary to 3 tablespoons of sweet cream. At the end of the bath, relax in a warm environment for an hour.

- **Contraindications**

At the recommended doses, it has no contraindications, except in pregnancy and breastfeeding. Keep out of the reach of children under 3 years of age.

Myrrh

It belongs to the resin family and, in fact, is associated with incense and gold, recalling the legend of the Magi and the gifts they brought to Jesus after his birth.

The supply difficulties and the commercial hoarding made it, in fact, a precious gift.

The ancient history books mention it up to more than 3,000 years ago. It has been used for centuries as a component of incense for religious purposes. The Egyptians used it, as well as in sun worship rites, also in embalming processes, in mixtures with other essential oils.

In ancient Greece myrrh was widely used, up to mixing it with wine and a mythological episode tells of its origin, linking it to Myrrh, daughter of the king of Cyprus, who for having had incestuous relationships with her father, was transformed by Aphrodite into a tree from the scented resin. From this union after nine months the tree-woman gave birth to Adonis.

Its astringent, disinfectant and healing properties have been known for centuries. The ancients used to carry myrrh paste with them into battle to spread on wounds.

Egyptian women used it in face masks against wrinkles, as they still do in Africa and Arab countries.

Israelis put powdered myrrh directly on the toothbrush as toothpaste.

In traditional Chinese medicine it is used as a healing remedy for sores and hemorrhoids and in menstrual cycle problems, such as amenorrhea.

Today it is present in almost all European national pharmacopoeias.

- Part used: resinoid.
- Extraction method: steam distillation.
- Base note: warm, spicy, bitter, balsamic scent.

- **Harmonizing**

This oil is highly valued in aromatherapy as a sedative, antidepressant and as a promoter of spiritual feelings. Myrrh serves to balance the spiritual world with the material one, giving us strength and optimism, especially helps people who are afraid to reveal their feelings.

It makes us humble and devoted, preparing us to receive energy and love from others. It helps to overcome the fear of death and the pain of separation. Queen of emotional blocks and our inability to live spiritually, it stimulates us especially during sleep by eliminating all excesses in us.

- **Contraindications**

Myrrh essential oil is non-irritating, does not cause sensitization and is non-toxic at low doses. Use sparingly. It is absolutely to be avoided its internal use during pregnancy and breastfeeding. Myrrh, in high doses, can cause sweating, nausea, vomiting and rapid heartbeat.

Ylang Ylang

Known for its numerous properties, it has a calming, hypotensive and aphrodisiac action, also useful as a tonic and astringent. In case of nervous tension, stress, agitation, high blood pressure, palpitations and tachycardia, the essential oils contained have a sedative effect on the nervous system and at the same time are tonic and stimulate circulation, with hypotensive effects. For therapeutic use it is good to make sure that the quality of the essential oil is extra or first grade.

The name ylang-ylang of Tagalog origin, means flower of flowers, or from ilang-ilan, meaning "uncommon", referring to the very particular aroma. The women of those places used to dissolve a few drops in coconut oil to protect skin and hair during the rainy season. Already the French colonists called it "aphrodisiac perfume", because it was used in harems together with other essential oils.

- A seemingly delicate flower, ylang-ylang is also called "the jasmine of the poor" because its fragrant petals are instead very resistant and allow for up to 6 successive distillations.

With about 60 kg of flowers, 1 kg of essential oil is obtained. The fresh and delicate flowers of the Ylang-Ylang tree are hand-picked early in the morning and distilled within hours. The distillation takes approximately 15 to 20 hours.

There are 6 types of different fragrances based on the distillation times:
- Ylang-Ylang Extra Superiéur - after a quarter of an hour.
- Ylang-Ylang Extra - after one hour.
- Ylang-Ylang I - after another hour.
- Ylang-Ylang II - up to the 6th hour.
- Ylang-Ylang III - until the 12th hour.
- Full Ylang-Ylang - at the end of the 20th hour.

The product of the first distillation is called ylang-ylang extra and is commonly used in perfumery. Subsequent distillations have a gradually lower quality.
The third distillation still maintains a fair amount of perfume and is used in soaps and personal hygiene products.

- Part used: flowers.
- Extraction method: steam distillation.
- Heart note: sweet, floral, spicy scent. The intoxicating strength of the aroma has a powerful liberating effect and is therefore of great help in problems of repression of femininity, to drive away uncertainties, to dissolve disappointments and free blocked feelings. Calm, unwind and relax.

- **Calming**

If inhaled, it has a relaxing action on the nervous system, reducing its disturbances, such as anxiety, depression, irritability, nervousness and insomnia. Ylang ylang essential oil creates harmony in case of contrasts, anger, resentment and frustration, because it promotes understanding and forgiveness, dissolves disappointments and offenses, restores the desire to love.

- **Hypotensive**

The essence is able to lower blood pressure and to mitigate the disturbances caused on the cardio-circulatory system by stress, such as palpitations and tachycardia. Take 1 drop of essence twice a day; dry inhalations with 1 drop on a handkerchief to be sniffed several times during the day.

- **Aphrodisiac**

It is an erotic essential oil, useful for awakening the senses, in case of frigidity, impotence, and for those who cannot let go; drives away doubt, insecurities and blocked feelings.
It is of great help in repressed femininity because it releases joy, sensuality, euphoria and internal security.

- **Toning and astringent for the skin**

It is indicated in case of excessive sebum production and acne; if diluted a few drops in the face cleanser, the dermis recovers tone and luminosity. If poured in small doses, in coconut oil or Shea butter, it is an excellent nourisher and protector for hair, subject to salt, wind and sun.

- **Relaxing bath**

10 drops in the bath water, emulsify by shaking the water vigorously, then immerse yourself for 20 minutes. After going outside, massage temples and forehead with 1 drop of essential oil in half a spoonful of apricot oil.

- **Shower**

3-4 drops on a wet sponge glove; gently massage the whole body.

- **Contraindications**

For external use only. Ylang ylang essential oil is a well tolerated oil but the rules of the skin test apply to ascertain any individual sensitivities, avoid internal use and during pregnancy, breastfeeding and on small children. Due to its intense fragrance, it should be used in moderation because it can cause nausea and headaches. Being a very intense essence it can cause skin allergies.

Neroli

Neroli essential oil is a vegetable oil produced by distillation of bitter orange blossoms. Its scent resembles that of bergamot. Sweet scent of the flower and bitter taste of the fruit characterize the bitter variety of orange. The essential oil of neroli is extracted from the flowers of the bitter orange which differs from the sweet variety due to its longer thorns, their darker colour, the more intense aroma of the leaves and flowers, the more colored and rougher skin of the fruit, but above all for the particular bitter taste of the pulp. This double aspect is also found in love and for this reason neroli essential oil has always been its symbol. Known for its numerous properties, it has a calming, rebalancing and regenerating action, useful against stress and menstrual pain.

The scent of neroli essential oil is sweet, honeyed, with slightly metallic and spicy facets. It is a less floral scent than that of the classic orange blossom. Neroli is one of the expensive essential oils, because it takes a ton of orange blossom to make a liter of essence.

Neroli is one of the few essential oils that has been scientifically proven to increase the production of serotonin in the brain. Serotonin is an important neurotransmitter and is capable of altering mood; in fact, when it is present at high levels, it increases our feeling of serenity and well-being.

It is one of the most used floral essences for the composition of countless perfumes. This fame derives mainly from the fact that it blends well with all citrus essences and floral notes thanks to its lunar predominance.

The essential oil of bitter orange blossoms was the favorite fragrance of Annamaria di Tremoville, wife of Flavio Orsini, count of the feud of Nerola, in Lazio in the second half of the 1500s. The chronicles narrate that the woman, of French origin, brought the beloved essential oil to her native land, giving it the name of "Neroli", in memory of her husband's village. It is associated with purity and perhaps due to the symbolism that derives from white flowers, it was formerly used to make the crown that encircled the head of brides during weddings, which served a dual purpose: to symbolize virginity and to ease possible worry and fear of the penetration that a young bride could feel towards her wedding night.

- Part used: flowers.
- Method of extraction: enfleurage.
- Heart note: warm, sweet, floral scent.

- **Rebalancing on the nervous system**

Neroli essential oil is indicated after mental fatigue and psychic tension, against fear, anxiety disorders, depression and calms thoughts in times of confusion. Bring peace to your heart, cheerfulness and comforting optimism. In afflictions it helps us to lighten its burden.

It strengthens us in situations where we see no way out. It exerts an effective calming action in case of emotional disturbances, nervousness, insomnia, hypertension, tachycardia, stress. It reconciles sleep and is very useful in case of overexcited children who fall asleep with difficulty.

Apply 2 drops of neroli essential oil (diluted, on delicate skins, in a little almond oil) on the inner surface of the wrists and rub them vigorously against each other, while raising the arms upwards, to better inhale the aroma that is released, through deep breathing. In case of emotional shocks, fears, stress, dilute 3 drops of essential oil in a teaspoon of almond oil and massage a little on the central part of the sternum. In case of mild depression, insomnia, anxiety, take an aromatic bath by pouring 8 drops of neroli essential oil and 8 drops of lavender essential oil on 3 handfuls of unrefined sea salt; add the mix to the hot tub water.

Alternatively, receive a massage on the whole back performed with flavored sesame oil in the following proportions: for 50 ml of vegetable oil add 6 drops of neroli essential oil, 5 drops of geranium essential oil and 5 drops of myrrh essential oil.

This essence is comparable to the "Rescue Remedy" in Dr. Bach flowers, as it helps us overcome fears, traumas, shocks and depressions.

- **Calming**

Useful in the treatment of psychosomatic disorders affecting the digestive system (cramps, digestive disorders of nervous origin, irritable bowel, meteorism), because it releases the muscles and relieves nervous tension. It is ideal for a relaxing massage and for massaging the belly in case of spasms, indigestion and menstrual pain. Add 15 drops of neroli to 100 ml of sweet almond oil to obtain a massage oil that eliminates stress and muscle tension.

- **Relaxing bath**

Mix 10 drops of neroli in the tub water, taking care to close the door and windows tightly to keep the vapors inside the bathroom and be able to breathe them.

- **Contraindications**

At the recommended doses, it has no contraindications. Keep out of the reach of children under 3 years of age.

Hyssop

Known for its numerous properties, it has a balsamic and expectorant action, useful against coughs, asthma and colds. Essential oil made with hyssop increases alertness and is a suitable tonic to gently ease the nerves in exhaustion, overwork, anxious states and nervous depression. Hyssop is one of those herbs known since ancient times, by the most ancient peoples, to the point that already in the Bible there is a reference as a cure for leprosy.

The ancient folk medicine recommended drinking the juice to expel the dead fetus in case of abortion. In the Middle Ages its beneficial properties on the lungs were already recognized and in the 9th century it was used for fumigations in the fight against plague epidemics. In the seventeenth century it was used for the preparation of an expectorant syrup to combat cough and various infectious conditions of the respiratory tract. The essential oil is extracted with the steam distillation method obtaining a yellow liquid with a spicy scent. Digestive, carminative, bechic, expectorant, the essential oil of Hyssop gives excellent results for treating respiratory system diseases, such as bronchitis, cough with phlegm, flu.

Good results are also obtained for digestive disorders and aerophagia.

- Part used: flowering tops.

- Extraction method: steam distillation.
- Heart Note: aromatic, spicy, fresh balsamic scent.

- **Invigorating**

Hyssop essential oil, if inhaled, gives support in case of emotional disorders such as anxiety and depression, stimulates the nervous system and is useful in case of psychophysical tiredness and stress.

- **Relaxing bath**

Pour 20 drops of hyssop essence into the bathtub and immerse yourself for 10 minutes, against tiredness and states of exhaustion.

- **Contraindications**

Hyssop essential oil should not be administered as such, because in small doses (2 grams) it can induce nausea, a feeling of malaise, psychic disturbances, convulsions and in some cases it can even be lethal. The use of Hyssop is strictly contraindicated in pregnancy, lactation and all children. Given its dangerousness, before using Hyssop it is good to ask your trusted herbalist for an opinion. Hyssop should not be taken together with anticonvulsant drugs and in any case, if you are following drug therapy, it is recommended to consult your doctor before taking this plant, which can modify the therapeutic effect of antidiabetic and immunodepressant drugs.

Some research tends to demonstrate that hyssop is able to stop the proliferation of HIV without harming the infected cells.

Rose

The rose, a flower with exceptional properties, is an extraordinary rebalancing agent capable of strengthening the nervous system, promoting digestion and reawakening sexuality. Spring stress, which occurs after months of work, affects the health of the body, absorbing our energies and causing a lowering of the immune system. Rose essential oil reduces anxiety attacks, the constant feeling of tension and agitation generated by stress and the consequent somatic manifestations. Known for its numerous properties, it carries out a balancing, soothing and harmonizing action, useful for self-esteem and against anxiety and wrinkles. The rose is the archetype of the flower and the symbol of both profane and divine love. Known for more than 3,000 years, ancient civilizations used it as a main ingredient in the manufacture of perfumes and cosmetics along with other essential oils. The Arabs and Berbers of Morocco have been distilling and producing rose water since the 1st century BC. C and used the infusion of its leaves for the anti-stress, tonic and antiseptic properties.

- The rose is one of the most difficult essences to distill, because it takes 4 to 5 tons of petals to obtain 1 kg of essential oil. In a drop of rose essential oil there is therefore the fragrance of about 30 roses; this low yield unfortunately justifies the high price of its essential oil. Rose essential oil is extracted from the Rosa damascena botanical species. Given the high costs of rose essential oil, there is no shortage of already diluted solutions on the market.

The harvest begins from mid-May to mid-June, at 4 in the morning and ends at 9; after this time, in fact, it becomes too hot, so the subtle volatile parts of the rose would be partially lost. Rose essential oil is one of those essential oils which, at room temperature, gels; otherwise, when heated, it returns to a liquid state. This also determines the evidence of the genuineness of the real rose essential oil.

- Part used: flower petals.
- Method of extraction: extraction in solvent.
- Heart note: floral, soft, delicate scent.

- **Harmonizing**

When inhaled, it opens and strengthens the heart. Rose essential oil relaxes the soul and activates the disposition for tenderness and love, as it develops patience, devotion and self-esteem. Gives joy and banishes negative thoughts, balancing negative emotions caused by anger, jealousy and stress. The scent of the essence is a wonderful psychological and physical support during pregnancy: excellent for accompanying women during childbirth and welcoming the new arrival with sweetness and love. In menopause it helps to soothe sadness and depression. In case of nervous depression, take 2 drops of rose essence twice a day.

- **Balancing of the female hormonal system**

If massaged on the stomach, it calms spasms in case of menstrual pain and stops bleeding. Indicated in disorders related to hormonal imbalances, anxiety and irritability that characterize premenstrual syndrome and menopause. To stimulate liver function, dilute 2 drops in 1 tablespoon of sweet almond oil and gently massage the liver area for a few minutes without pressing, just making a light circular rubbing to let the oil penetrate.

- **Stress reliever**

4 drops of rose essential oil diluted in a spoonful of jojoba oil and applied to the center of the forehead, under the chin and around the navel, with a circular message repeated three times: here is an excellent strategy to combat stress. To complete and amplify the relaxing effect of the message, you can drink a cup of rose tea.

- **Invigorating**

Against sexual asthenia, useful for a couple's massage or for a relaxing bath with an aphrodisiac effect; it is the oil of love and eroticism, because it enhances inner beauty and mitigates conflicts by instilling peace and happiness. Prepare a massage oil by diluting 2 drops of rose essential oil and 2 drops of jasmine in 2 tablespoons of sweet almond oil.

- **Environmental diffusion**

1 drop for every square meter of the environment in which it spreads, by means of an essential oil burner, or in radiator humidifiers.

- **Aromatherapy bath**

10 drops of rose essential oil or, for an even more relaxing effect, 3 drops each of rose, ylang-ylang and sandalwood essential oils added to the hot tub water will eliminate anxiety, tension and stress, and will promote night rest.

- **Massage oil**

In 200 ml of sweet almond oil put 20 drops of essential oil, massage the body during pregnancy or in case of stretch marks and dry skin.

- **Contraindications**

At the recommended doses, it has no contraindications. Not suitable for children under 3 years of age, pregnant or breastfeeding women.

Himalayan flowers for the second chakra

Himalayan Flower Enhancers directly affect the various energy levels controlled by the Chakras, removing negative feelings and stimulating positive ones. The Himalayan Flower Enhancers were identified by Tanmaya in 1990, during a stay of several months in a Himalayan valley. The term Enhancers means catalysts, because the essences are not only remedies aimed at working on negative emotions and inner states but also favor very deep processes of energy rebalancing and spiritual development to bring to light qualities buried within the person. They can be taken pure alone or diluted together with Bach flowers or other flowers.

Tanmaya's first preparations involved nine combinations, seven directly connected to the plexuses, better known by the Indian name of chakra plus a general catalyst and a flower particularly suitable for children; subsequently their number multiplied with the discovery of new flowers, suitable for modulating specific emotions.

They are Flowers with a very rapid and powerful effect, unlike Bach Flowers, which are among the slowest and most delicate; this power is sometimes very useful, other times it can represent a risk of excessive action. While the Bach Flowers can be considered mainly emotional remedies, i.e. aimed at rebalancing human emotions, the Himalayan Flowers, thanks to the nature of the soil on which they grow, essentially address the spiritual dimension of man, stimulating the need for prayer, of meditation and connection with the divine that dwells in him.

Himalayan floral essences are liquid extracts that contain the energy of the flower to be administered generally orally, and can also be used in bath water, sprayed on the body or in the environment, or combined with oil for massage.

Well Being

It favors the relationship with the Hara, with one's own center. Stimulates creativity and coordinates emotions. The second Chakra is an energy reservoir and the center for basic energy transformation. Well Being helps dissolve accumulated anger, birth traumas, fear of death, emotional instability.

It happens, in certain life situations, to have emotional instability, lack of trust, anxiety, fear of death and annihilation, to no longer feel good in the place where we were until recently, in which our harmony with world seems to screech. The fear of death can become a phobia that affects our lives, produces anxiety, anguish, instability, depression, apathy and indifference, resulting in the loss of self-esteem and trust in others and in the world. We tend to put things off, to be in a bad mood.

It also happens that we have difficulty letting something or someone into our lives, a relationship, money, a job, a change, we are caught up in fears, anxiety.

It frequently happens that we have great difficulty letting go of the old, the past, what is objectively no longer part of our lives and which anchors us to a past from which we find it hard to detach ourselves: from a finished relationship, to objects that no longer part of our present, of friends who no longer have anything to do with us, of habits. In all these cases our second chakra, seat of our Ki, center of transformation of basic energy, is weak or altered, has energy blocks. The balance of the relationship between the inner world and the outer world has been broken.

Well Being helps to center oneself, stimulates creativity and coordinates emotions. Promotes and stimulates personal power, helps to rebalance around one's center and find balance. The dosage for taking the essences, pure or diluted, is two drops under the tongue several times a day

It helps to regulate the flow of emotions, to rediscover harmony, to have a correct relationship with the past and with the present, with letting go and welcoming. The second chakra is an energy reservoir and the center for basic energy transformation. Helps dissolve accumulated anger, birth trauma, fear of death, emotional instability.

Californian flowers for the second chakra

The Californian Flowers extend the Bach Flowers.
Richard Kats and Patricia Kaminski, founders of the FES (Flower Essence Society), together with the work of other researchers have discovered more than 150 flowers since 1979. They work on more modern and current specific problems which at the time Bach lived did not they were so preponderant or they weren't talked about like today: anorexia and bulimia, sexual disorders, diseases deriving from environmental pollution. It is possible to create composite essences by combining Bach and Californian flowers, as well as essences from other flower therapy repertoires from other parts of the world. Californian flower remedies are prepared in the same simple way as Bach flowers, by placing wild flower corollas in a glass bowl filled with spring water and leaving them to infuse in the sun for a few hours. This liquid, very rich in vital force, is then filtered, diluted in brandy and used for the preparation of the so-called stock bottles (or concentrates).

The choice of essences, as with Bach flowers, is always personalized and in relation to the mood and emotions you want to rebalance. Once the remedy or remedies indicated for the personal problem have been chosen, two drops of each are poured into a small bottle with a 30 ml dropper, filled with natural mineral water and two teaspoons of brandy as a preservative.

The dosage is 4 drops 4 times a day, for a period of a few weeks or in any case until the symptoms improve or disappear.

Being a completely natural and non-toxic cure, they have no contraindications, do not cause side effects, can be combined without problems with both traditional and homeopathic medicines (of which they are considered complementary) or other flower therapy remedies.

Basil

For those who tend to separate sexuality from spirituality not considering it possible to integrate them, while in reality they are different expressions of the same energy. This problem is more evident in relationships where there is an urgent need to seek sexual intercourse outside the couple's relationship. This can lead to consequences such as seeking clandestine sexual relations outside the couple because they are considered sinful. Strong attraction to pornography and illicit forms of sexuality. In the unconscious struggle to reconcile these forces, the soul often gives up or becomes ensnared with degrading sexual activity.

The essence helps to live the person in his entirety, made up of instincts and spirituality, as sacred. Useful remedy for people tormented by fixations, sexual obsessions, blocks or for couples who have problems of sexual understanding.

Calla Lily

For those who are confused about their sexual identity.
For those born of a different sex from what their parents wanted.
Desire to belong to the opposite sex.
The flower makes one accept one's sexual identity.
It is the essence that allows you to integrate male and female energies, dissolves confusion about sexual orientation, allowing for a harmonious development of the personality through the clear and serene expression of sexuality. It is also useful for those people who are unable to adapt to social conventions relating to sexuality, who experience homosexual tendencies in a conflictual way, or who cannot find a clear identity because they have homosexual and heterosexual tendencies at the same time. The lack of sexual identity not only affects the body with frustrations and inhibitions, but creates a deep inner torment that can make interpersonal relationships difficult.
Calla Lily teaches the individual that true masculine and feminine qualities are found united within themselves, rather than externally in physical or biological traits. In this way the personality evolves towards a greater balance and a harmonious expression of the soul. For teenagers who find it difficult to relate to boys of the same gender.

Easter Lily

People in conflict with their sexuality, who live it in a degraded and dirty way. It is difficult for them to reconcile spirituality and sexuality.

This can lead to abstinence or tend towards perversion and promiscuity. Very important remedy for women. The white Easter Lily has always been a symbol of both purity and sexuality and reproduction, it is extremely conflicting for the individual to integrate the sexual life with the spiritual life. For good reason, many spiritual paths require celibacy as a condition of spiritual development, it is possible, however, for modern people to reconcile these apparent opposites; which will bring forth new and important possibilities. Easter Lily is an important remedy to help those people who feel great inner tension between sexuality and spirituality. These conflicts can express themselves in one direction or the other, towards a promiscuity which degrades and damages the astral body or towards a bigotry which separates the person from the vital energies of the lower body. Easter Lily is a particularly important remedy for women and can help with impurities and problems with the sexual and reproductive organs.

Easter Lily's most fundamental gift is to enable the individual to fully utilize the psychic energy currents associated with the sexual and reproductive organs.

Hibiscus

For women who have a negative image of sexuality due to abuse or violence suffered.

For men who have distorted images of women, to establish a more positive relationship with female sexuality. The flower gives warmth to the body and soul, especially taking care of sexuality. When the person fails to live the instinctual and passionate aspect of her being serenely and with spontaneous sweetness, sexual expression is cold, detached or blocked. This flower gives women awareness, acceptance and authentic expression of their sexuality, in harmony with the deepest and purest feelings of her heart.

When there is a decline in sexual desire after menopause. For those women who experience sexuality with little warmth and desire, who avoid intimate relationships and chronically have little predisposition to initiate actions that lead to sexual pleasure. They cannot make their sex a place of pleasure. They experience it as an obligation.

The flower helps to learn to enjoy sexuality.

Sticky Monkeyflower

For those who are afraid of intimacy and sexuality understood as deep contact with each other. Often these people can mask their fear by seeking lots of sexual intercourse that does not involve true heartfelt sympathy, or on the contrary they avoid any kind of sexual contact. This flower helps integrate the physical and spiritual aspects of love. People dominated by the fear of demonstrating their true feelings and being discovered by others in their affections.

For those who repress themselves, they self-censor; those who would like to express their feelings of love and are unable to do so and therefore fall into loneliness. On many occasions, their blocks are due to unprocessed sorrows in previous relationships. The flower gives warmth in the intimate relationship, security, expressiveness, adjustment, clarity, acceptance, joy and depth in the affections. The lesson that makes learning is to have the courage to show true feelings, learn to understand the meaning of sexual activity.

It can be of great help in adolescence to overcome embarrassment and shyness related to sexual feelings and desires. Through sexuality one can enter into deep contact with another human being and thus experience the strongest ecstasy and the greatest pain of the soul.

So the fear in these people is to expose their ego to another human being of being vulnerable or rejected.

This is why sexuality is superficial and devoid of real participation.
In menopause it is useful for developing new models of intimacy, transforming sexual identity by making it part of the passage of menopause.

Australian flowers for the second chakra

The Australian Bush Flowers are today 69 plus 19 essences created by the combination of Australian Flowers and were introduced by Ian White, Australian biologist and psychologist. They are not yet well known and used in Italy by the general public, but they are highly appreciated by flower therapists and we find Australian flowers included in many herbal and homeopathic complexes. They are among the most powerful and widely used flowers after Bach Flowers, they have a very high energy, one of the highest among floral remedies. Australian Aborigines have always used Flowers to treat discomfort or emotional imbalances, as was the case in ancient Egypt, India, Asia and South America.

The dose, for both adults and children, consists of seven drops to be taken twice a day (morning and evening) under the tongue, or in a little water. The essences should be taken for about twenty days or a month, except for particularly powerful essences.

Being a completely natural and non-toxic cure, they have no contraindications, do not cause side effects, can be combined without problems with both traditional and homeopathic medicines (of which they are considered complementary) or other flower therapy remedies. You can prepare a single remedy (whose action will then be particularly "targeted", deep and fast), or mix different remedies together; in this case it is advisable not to exceed 4 or 5 essences and, if possible, try to choose flowers with similar and synergistic properties to treat a specific problem.

Australian flowers are also very effective when applied to the skin and can be added to creams, gels, massage oils, medicated ointments or diluted in bath water. For a topical treatment, the recommended quantity is about 7 drops of each chosen remedy, to be mixed in half a cup of cream; instead, 15–20 drops of each essence should be poured into the bathtub.

The duration of treatment always depends on the individual response. A positive reaction is often obtained in about two weeks and on average two months are sufficient to rebalance numerous psychophysical problems. Some particularly "powerful" flowers (such as, for example, Waratah) usually exert a very rapid action, even in a few days. Many times, after resolving an inner discomfort or conflict, other emotional imbalances can emerge, which will gradually be treated with the corresponding flowers.

Flannel Flower

For those who do not like physical contact with others and are not comfortable with their physical and emotional intimacy. For those who find it difficult to express their feelings in words. The flower helps the discovery of the ability to enjoy all physical manifestations and in particular sensitivity to physical contact with others and the reduction of one's boundaries. Renew confidence in expressing and revealing yourself to others, through sensuality and sweetness. This essence defines a characteristic floral psychological type where the person shows a difficulty in getting in touch with the body. This leads him to avoid physical contact and to be stingy in giving and receiving strokes. They are people who normally appear different from what they really are, in fact they seem to have the possibility of great gestures of affection. Instead this is not real and if the caresses are present they are forced or the internal experience that accompanies them is shallow.

It is about seduction which is normally a narcissistic personality trait and not a real interest in the other. It is also common to find a block that hinders the free expression of affects.

The main function of this essence is to give the ability to enjoy body contact, to be free in the expression of feelings, tender and to feel skin-to-skin contact positively. For those who do not like physical contact with others and are not comfortable with their physical and emotional intimacy.

For those who find it difficult to express their feelings in words. The flower helps the discovery of the ability to enjoy all physical manifestations and in particular sensitivity to physical contact with others and the reduction of one's boundaries. Renew confidence in expressing and revealing yourself to others, through sensuality and sweetness. This essence defines a characteristic floral psychological type where the person shows a difficulty in getting in touch with the body. This leads him to avoid physical contact and to be stingy in giving and receiving strokes. They are people who normally appear different from what they really are, in fact they seem to have the possibility of great gestures of affection. Instead this is not real and if the caresses are present they are forced or the internal experience that accompanies them is shallow. It is about seduction which is normally a narcissistic personality trait and not a real interest in the other. It is also common to find a block that hinders the free expression of affects.

The main function of this essence is to give the ability to enjoy body contact, to be free in the expression of feelings, tender and to feel skin-to-skin contact positively.

She Oak

The major function of the remedy is related to the emotional factors that inhibit the fertility of the woman. It is beneficial for those women who have problems getting pregnant, despite having no physical pathologies. Also useful for women who have premenstrual syndrome or irregular cycles or in the menopause period. It has different dosages with respect to the various problems.

This essence describes a person who has imbalances in the feminine aspects. They are women who generally tend to cover or hide their feminine aspects, their ability to seduce, their physical forms. They have often had problems in their relationship with their mother and motherhood becomes a difficult compromise to deal with. If they have daughters, they have problems with them and have difficulty understanding them and often a problem of competitiveness can arise. Another important trait is the lack of confidence in the creative abilities that the woman may have and this emotional block manifests itself with sterility, such as the inability to conceive, even if there are no known causes for this. It is very useful in women who feel incapable and fearful of having their first child.

The essence is also very useful in cases where an internal conflict combined with a strong unconscious fear of sexual pleasure and the belief of being an unworthy person generates feelings of shame and guilt that hinder the freedom necessary to reach orgasm.

The uterus is the matrix that represents the female identity and her creative capacity in the body.

Problems, confusions and dysfunctions in this area indicate the presence of conflicts with being a woman that have an intimate relationship with one's experience of femininity. In the case of men, She Oak works on insecurities and doubts about the male condition and the fear of losing manhood.

She Oak is also useful for water retention that characterizes the menstrual cycle, and as hormone replacement therapy in menopause.

Bach flowers for the second chakra

Bach flowers are an alternative medicine created by the British doctor Edward Bach, born on 24 September 1886 in Moseley from a Welsh family in England. He graduated in medicine in 1912 and immediately worked in the emergency room of the university hospital where he began to be noticed for the large amount of time he devoted to patients. He was immediately critical of other doctors, who studied the disease as if it were separate from the individual, without focusing on the patients themselves.

It is well known that our emotional states have a profound influence on our well-being and health. An altered emotional state that repeats itself every day creates real dysfunctions in our body.

Ninety per cent of the causes of human disease come from planes beyond the physical, and it is on these planes that symptoms begin to manifest before the physical body shows any disturbance. If we can identify the negative moods that crop up when we get sick, we can fight the disease better and heal faster. Using floral remedies you try to influence the deeper structures from which the disease originates. Bach flowers rebalance the emotions. They address only and exclusively how we react emotionally to the vicissitudes, experiences and problems in our days. They give great serenity and peace, courage or strength, they help us feel at the fullest of our possibilities.

They can be useful in the face of an illness, not from a physical point of view but just as a mood support. The person is seen as a complete individual where emotions are a pivotal point, and not just as a physical body with symptoms. It is therefore necessary to analyze the emotional state and not the physical symptoms, based on this the suitable remedies are found. In fact subjects with identical physical problems react and live with different emotions and feelings. Bach flowers have no contraindications and do not interact with medicines.

Bach has thus divided the 38 flowers from which the remedies are drawn. The very first flowers discovered by Bach were the so-called "12 Healers", which the Welsh doctor promptly began to experiment first on himself and then on his patients; the other 26 were discovered a short time later, divided into "7 Helpers" and "19 Assistants". Dr Bach later abandoned the distinction between 'Healers', 'Helpers' and 'Assistants' as superfluous, but many people around the world still use it. Bach Flowers do not help to repress negative attitudes, but transform them into their positive side. The Bach Flowers associated with the first chakra are only in general, because the flowers must still be chosen based on the emotion that is not in harmony and must be balanced.

Rock Rose

It belongs to the category of "Healers".
Who needs this flower is a person who is easily frightened, at the ringing of a telephone, a bell, the fall of a book, a bottle, the scream of a person, an animal, the siren of a ambulance, in the presence of the police. Usually this person is not fearful, but over time the accumulation of various shocks begins to create real panic attacks.
The positive state of Rock Rose makes the individual strong and courageous, in the blocked state, despite the fact that the person knows how to behave in the face of an emergency, he freezes, his energies are blocked, he is afraid bordering on terror and cannot to think and act in a useful way. The floral remedy acts immediately in dangerous situations, it is instantaneous, it blocks terror and does not make you lose control. Rock Rose gives energy and restores a correct nervous balance even after particularly stressful events.
Very useful in sudden anxiety attacks.
With Rock Rose, safety and courage allow you to take any initiative, even in rescue situations.
Rock Rose, gives courage in facing emergency situations, helps to drive away fear, acts quickly on the solar plexus by dissolving anxiety, unlocks the fear of the moment, helps not to lose one's head in times of crisis, and makes one face the situation calmly and courageously.

Gives rapid emotional improvement in emergency situations, helps to live better with one's nervous temperament, gives immediate courage, courage in facing emergency situations, helps to push away fear, unlocks fear of the moment, helps not to lose the head in moments of crisis, and makes you face the situation calmly and courageously.

Mimulus

It belongs to the category of "Healers".
Who needs this flower is a person who sees dangers everywhere, is often anxious, fearful and has a great imagination that does not coincide with reality. This state of mind can arise after many frightening events or as a result of particular situations such as an economic crisis, clearly the person begins to live in apprehension fearing losing the house, the car, the land.
Fears in Mimulus are specific and precise.
The strong sensitivity to the surrounding world makes one tremble easily, such as, for example, when one has to speak in public or in any case in any "excessive" situation where there is too much noise, too much light, too many people. This Flower should also be administered for particular fears such as: tunnel, bridge, height, darkness, open and closed space, because to all intents and purposes they are certain fears. Mimulus is the remedy to stimulate that calm courage and strength that are hidden in these people, so that they can face the daily trials of life with firmness.
With Mimulus you are sure, and you go towards the world with calm, courage and strength, taking into account your own sensitivity.

Cherry Plum

It belongs to the category of "Assistants".
Cherry Plum is one of the group remedies that Dr. Bach defined for Fear. The Cherry Plum type fear is very specific and is the fear that you are losing control of yourself and that you might do something horrible, such as harming others or thinking about suicide (in this case, notify your Doctor immediately treating).
When you are afraid of losing control of your body and mind, you are impulsive and out of control. You are afraid of harming others. It is about to explode. In the Cherry Plum state you feel like a pressure cooker, or you do things you don't want to do, or you have compulsive attitudes such as: continuous shopping, smoking, drinking. Applying yourself to manual activities certainly relieves the extreme tension you feel. With Cherry Plum you are able to manage your energy with confidence and spontaneity. Every situation is a source of strength and ability.
The floral remedy acts immediately in situations of strong agitation, it is instantaneous; blocks the fear of losing control. The person will immediately feel a sense of tranquility and serenity, driving the obsessive thoughts away from the mind.

Aspen

It belongs to the category of "Assistants".

Who needs this flower is a person very sensitive to negative energies, usually transmitted from the outside. Aspen is for all undefined and vague fears; that of the dark, of magic, of monsters. Suitable for all people who have a particular sensitivity. When problems are experienced even before they occur. Very suitable for children's fears. Poplar leaves shake easily, a breath of air is enough for them to move. Thus people who need Aspen are sensitive to their surroundings; bad news, other people's illnesses are perceived as their own. The floral remedy immediately stops the fantasy generated by fear, calms the person giving them optimism, makes them understand that fear was only the fruit of the mind. Furthermore, if a similar state of mind were to recur in life, he will now be able to understand what to do and therefore be able to simply say: I have to stop listening to or reading negative news.

With Aspen your sensitivity becomes a source of security, you increase your courage.

Red Chestnut

It belongs to the category of "Assistants".
Who needs this flower is a person who cares excessively for loved ones.
This worry or fear becomes chronic when the thought that something bad could happen to a loved one (child, husband, partner, colleague, animal) becomes fixed, this condition in the long run can cause insomnia.
This person constantly watches over their loved ones and their lives, trying to change it to their own taste and liking, unknowingly creating numerous problems and inconveniences. It would seem the classic flower of apprehensive parents, in fact it is, but not only for parents but for all those who are afraid that something will happen to their loved ones. The slightest delay or the slightest sneeze immediately puts you in a state of excessive agitation. It allows you to break the umbilical cord that binds us to people or situations. The Remedy helps people who find themselves in this state of mind to think of their loved ones in a serene and calm way, so that, instead of communicating anxiety, they are of comfort and help.
With Red Chestnut you live a free and safe life, you develop a great helping force towards others.

Rescue Remedy

By combining two or more flowers together, personalized blends can be obtained, i.e. aimed at a particular and subjective need.

However, there is a combination prepared by Bach himself for general use; it is the emergency remedy called Rescue Remedy, a mixture of five flowers, which according to Bach would be useful in more acute situations: extreme stress, panic attacks, fainting, bad news, but also physical traumas.

As well as by mouth, this remedy can also be applied to the temples or wrists, or directly to the painful area.

It consists of a blend of:

- Star of Bethlehem, against sudden shock.
- Rock Rose, against panic or terror.
- Impatiens, to restore calm.
- Clematis, against the tendency to sag, the feeling of pulling away just before passing out.
- Cherry Plum, against the fear of losing control, of going crazy.

It is the only remedy which, as a rule, is not prepared exclusively in liquid form, but also in lactose tablets and ointments. In the latter formulation, called "Rescue Cream" Crab Apple is added, the purification remedy, for its purifying effect; it can be useful on various occasions: traumas, small skin rashes, muscle pain and tension, dehydrated skin.

It is very useful, for example, in children, for small sudden fears, in cases of accidents, when receiving bad news (mourning, illness), sudden moments of anxiety, fears, panic attacks. Put 4 drops of Rescue Remedy in a glass of water and sip it; initially with small sips close together (even every two or three minutes), then as the symptoms subside, the number of intakes is reduced. If you don't have the availability or don't have the time to take a glass of water, you can take 4 drops of the pure remedy.

The Rescue is an emergency remedy, and should be used as such. It cannot replace the daily use of Bach flowers. To obtain good results and to be in good health with flower therapy, it is important to hire the most suitable flowers for each one, personalizing them on the basis of the current situation.

Wild Oat

It belongs to the "Aid" category.

Who needs this flower is a person who never finds satisfaction in everything he thinks or does. He always has a thousand ideas to put into action, many intuitions and in the end only indecisions, he continually decides and also takes the initiative but while executing it he changes his mind again, project or other. His dissatisfaction can be seen in all its aspects. Indecision is generalized, not between two things. When choosing from a multitude of possibilities is difficult, Wild Oat helps you get your way. Classic example of the young person faced with the choice of the right school when all or many seem suitable. You would like to do something important but you don't know what. Wild Oat allows you to get in touch with your own skills and intuition.

The state of indecision of the Wild Oat type is different from that of the Scleranthus type, because in the second case the doubt is not about which direction to take, but rather about how to proceed or what to choose, despite having very clear the various alternatives. Wild Oat people, on the other hand, don't know what the possible alternatives are because they haven't yet clearly defined their goals. The remedy helps these people understand what their true role is, making them rediscover their life purpose, so that they can clearly understand which direction to go.

With Wild Oat you are able to do whatever you like, even if your interests are multiple, you know your destination.

Century

It belongs to the category of "Healers".
Centaury is the remedy for people who find it difficult to say no to others. They are good-natured and kind and love to help others. Sometimes, however, unscrupulous people take advantage of it and the individual Centaury finds himself, in spite of himself, a slave to the desires and will of others. The Centaury remedy does not numb the Centaury personality, but rather helps this type of person develop courage and self-determination so as to be able to say enough at the right time and not submit to the wishes and orders of others.

The lack of ability to impose one's own opinions and needs makes one weak, even physically. Often one is a Red Cross nurse and behind this great desire to help others hides one's inability to assert oneself and then complain that one feels exploited. This state of mind can arise in various situations: towards a child, towards a partner, a parent, or as a weakness towards a vice: such as cigarettes, sweets, food, expensive clothes, luxury cars, drugs, gambling, sex.

The essence helps the will and self-respect, gives energy, allows to be able to affirm one's personality and to have a balanced attitude towards others, gives the ability to give but without being overwhelmed. The new self-determination will restore vitality and zest for life.

With Centaury you know your values and your needs.

You are capable of integrating with others, but respecting your own uniqueness. The person with this disposition will gain energy, become more determined and will be able to express his opinion when necessary.

Star of Bethlehem

It belongs to the category of "Assistants".

Who needs this flower is a person who has received a shock: bad news, an accident, a bereavement, a disappointment, a trauma, a wound on the body, great frights, in short, an event for which the person is left without breath, as if frozen; in that precise moment he doesn't feel any reactions, he remains petrified.

Star of Bethlehem is one of the remedies that make up the Rescue Remedy. It is the remedy for any kind of shock, such as unexpected bad news or an unwanted and unexpected event. It can also be used for the effects of a shock many years ago, sometimes even the earliest in childhood. This remedy is also used for the sense of emptiness and loss that is sometimes felt when a loved one dies or moves away, as shock can be associated with these events. Star of Bethlehem is the Remedy that gives comfort in such circumstances.

Useful for mourning or traumatic situations, small or large, but which do not allow a free flow of one's energy.

With Star of Bethlehem, the necessary vital force is found, traumas are overcome and one feels one's soul consoled.

Number of the second chakra

The number associated with the second chakra is six, like the six petals of the lotus which represents it and which identifies the idea we have of creation: in the Bible the world was created in six days and Jewish tradition has it continue for six millennia.

Six is the number that represents responsibility and nurturing for family and community, as well as finding balance and harmony with our environment.

According to St. Augustine, six is the perfect number:

- "Six is a perfect number in itself, and not because God created the world in six days; rather the opposite is true. God created the world in six days because this number is perfect, and it would remain perfect even if the work of six days did not exist".

Even Kabbalah scholars agree on the importance of 6; in fact, the first word of the Bible, "Bereshit", translated as "in the beginning", numerically corresponds to the phrase "He created 6".

So, just as 4 is related to manifestation (the spirit that manifests itself in matter), 6 represents Creation ("God created Heaven and Earth, therefore he is already polarized), and the Seraphim, the most perfect angels created by God, they have 6 wings.

Furthermore, if 4 are the sides of a square, 6 are the faces of a cube, one the projection of the other, from the three-dimensional space to the two-dimensional plane.

Furthermore, since 6 is made up of 3+3, i.e. corresponding to two opposite triangles (think of the six-pointed star, or Solomon's seal), it represents duality: ascension and materialization, separation and union, altruism and selfishness, and also human nature and divine nature of Christ. Also in the Tarot, 6 is the number of choice, the lover at the crossroads between two women, to indicate ambivalence, and on a throne in the shape of a cube, which has 6 faces, sits the Emperor, an arcane number 4.

We also note that the six is almost exactly the ratio of the circumference to the radius (2π) and thus we arrive at the second symbol expressed by the chakra, or rather the circumference, as an emanation from the centre, which in the most universal sense represents the Principle, symbolized geometrically from the point, as arithmetically it is from the unit, which represents the manifestation, the creation, measured by the ray emanating from the Principle. Each ray defines a point on the circumference which symbolizes a being sprung from the creative energy of the center (and thus the "life force of the lingam" returns).

Creation, therefore, in the infinite multiplicity of all its forms generated by polarization, is symbolized by the infinite points that make up the circumference. The circle is also assimilated to the uroboric symbol of the snake biting its tail, also a cyclical symbol of evolution and eternal return, of the continuous recurrence of deaths and rebirths, in the inexhaustibility of creation. According to some psychological currents, the multifaceted totality expressed by the Uroboros represents the infinite facets of the unconscious very well.

The Uroboros therefore becomes a symbol of the unconscious itself, where everything is present at the same time and from which every single individuality (every point of the circumference) struggles to separate itself.

In this case we have: circle = unconscious, center = consciousness, i.e. a duality analogous to the one seen previously: circle = created, center = Creator, in turn analogous to the polarity inherent in the number 6 = 3+3 (male-female).

Affinity with other numbers:
- Fair: 3, 4, 5 and 8.
- Excellent: 1, 2 and 6.

We can associate each number with a planet, a zodiac sign and a fundamental element of life on Earth. For Number 6 we have:
- Sign: Virgo.
- Planet: Mercury.
- Element: Earth.

The archetype of number 6 is the Angel.
His Shadow Number is the Martyr.
The Martyr represents the shadow side of the Angel and represents the "internalized parent", predisposed to help others grow and evolve.

Central to this challenge is the need to offer love and support to others, yet avoid following the usual model of giving, never receiving anything in return. The tendency of the "Martyr" is to immerse himself in the role of savior, who always feels called upon to offer his help, even without anyone asking him, sometimes even in an inopportune way. The origin of the problem can be referred to affective deficiencies in the family.

The Martyr, in an attempt to please others to get their approval, continually sacrifices a part of himself and unconsciously attracts people with low self-esteem who, within a relationship, will tend to prove needy and consequently dependent. The challenge is to recognize this shadow with its characteristics and integrate it by restoring balance.

Having self-awareness can be the only way to integrate this shadow, recognize and accept it and then understand how to transform one's way of dealing with oneself and with others. It is primarily useful to recognize that the need to intervene in the lives of others is your need, so be certain that your help has really been requested and if it is, you will have to ascertain whether it is the result of a habit that you yourself have established, you will also have to correct these old habits that you have given to those close to you. Take a photo of when you were a child, place it in a place where it can often be seen and start talking to the most hidden part of you, your inner child.

Make the people close to you independent, by doing this the benefit will be mutual.

Phisical exercises

- **Exercise 1**

Relax, shake your arms and legs, sit on the floor with your back straight, and then do alternate breathing for a few minutes.

- **Exercise 2**

Assume the quadruped position and perform the "horse's back / cat's arched back" exercise 7 times.

- **Exercise 3**

Lie on your back and bend your legs keeping them closed.
The arms are extended horizontally with the palms facing up; slowly turn your head to the left at the same time as your legs to the right, until you reach maximum extension.
Turn your head and legs back to the center and turn them in the opposite direction as before (head to the right and legs to the left).
Repeat 7 times with slow, fluid motion, always remaining loose and relaxed.

- **Exercise 4**

Sit upright and place the back of your right hand on the back of your left hand, thumb tips touching.
Place your hands below your navel, palms facing down.
Close your eyes, inhale deeply through the nose and repeat the mantra "vam" repeatedly while exhaling, then inhale again through the nose repeating everything 7 times.

- **Exercise 5**

Lie on your back with your eyes closed and relax all the muscles of the body, concentrating on slow and progressive breathing.
Place your hands below the navel in the center of your belly and feel it rise and fall with your breath.
As you inhale, concentrate on assimilating prana and bringing it into the sacral chakra as you exhale.
With each breath, imagine an orange beam of energy flowing from your hands to your belly and spreading throughout your body.
Dwell on this image for 7 breath cycles.
Then place your hands back on the floor, palms down, and lie down for a few minutes.

- **Exercise 6**

Spread your legs so that the distance between your feet is shoulder width apart.

Move your pelvis back and forth by bending your knees slightly.
Repeat several times.
Now imagine finding yourself inside a cylinder and having to polish it with a movement of the hips.
With your hands on your hips, rotate your pelvis uniformly (as if you had to adhere perfectly to the internal surface of the cylinder).

- **Exercise 7**

Sit cross-legged on the floor.
Grab your ankles with both hands and inhale deeply.
Arch your spine forward and lift your torso; rotate the upper part of the pelvis backwards.
As you exhale, arch your spine back and bring your pelvis forward.
Repeat several times, pronouncing a mantra if you like.

Stones for the 2st Chakra

In crystallotherapy stones of the 2nd Chakra are considered those whose color varies from dark red to orange, of any type of brightness or transparency. The minerals of this color have a revitalizing effect and allow the subject to find balance and serenity.

They regulate blood circulation and metabolism. The area of placement of the stones is the region above the pubic bone.

The range of the orange colored minerals:

- They act on the organs of digestion.
- Get rid of depressions.
- Reduce interpersonal problems.
- They support the vital processes of adjustment.
- They support blood circulation.
- Stimulate self-healing.
- They vitalize fertility and the sexual organs.

The crystals that can rebalance the second chakra are Coral, Carnelian, Tiger's Eye, Jade, Heliotrope, Selenite, Aragonite, Aventurine, Sunstone, Topaz.

Feel its energy passing through the sacral chakra as you hold it in your hand or wear it by ring or necklace. You don't have to buy them all, just choose the stones you prefer or which you already have. The color orange is not very suitable for people with too much energy, too nervous or agitated.

Coral

"Love and harmony".

Coral, as we know, is not part of the mineral world. Coral, in fact, is made up of communities of small polyps which form, at the base of their soft body, a calcium carbonate skeleton with a protective and supportive function. Since time immemorial, man has been looking for this marine gem as a symbol of beauty and a source of regenerating energy.

Characteristic or psychological problems disappear with the help of Coral, so that our life opens up to more collaborative and fulfilling experiences, where communication is not difficult and anxieties, suspicions and shyness appear further away and less limiting. Coral hardens the entire skeletal system and the body in general.

It exists in black, pink, red, white, blue (rare) variants. It gives off exceptional vibrations and in crystallotherapy it is linked to blood. Forms an energy shield that protects against negativity in general and some people. Associated with Turquoise it gives even more powerful protection as together they symbolize the four Elements. Stimulates energy exchange, making new energy (Prana) flow in place of the old one. It is relaxing and eliminates melancholy and worries. Strengthens personality and stimulates intuition. It awakens the stimulus and sexual attraction. Against nightmares. It is curative for many internal and external

ailments. Indicated for anemia, ulcer, constipation, inappetence, indigestion, obesity, asthma, cough, lowers fever, eye and spleen problems, stimulates the secretion of mucous membranes and bile, antihemorrhagic and healing, strengthens the heart and circulation (blood cells red), removes toxins, relieves arthritic pain, regulates the menstrual cycle.
Particularly:

- Red Coral is indicated for the vertebral column, herniated discs, osteoporosis, joint blockages, stimulates blood constitution, strengthens muscles, activates the thyroid and metabolism, fights stiff neck.
- Pink Coral instills good humour, regulates the functions of the pancreas and liver, the spleen, the thymus, the symphatic system.
- White and/or Blue Coral is useful for problems relating to nerve and brain tissue and as a bone tonic (white).
- Black Coral stimulates an essential distrust in those who are too naive towards others, helps when one feels betrayed or exploited, increases attention span and learning.

Carnelian

The term carnelian derives from the Latin "carnis," which means "flesh", a stone so called due to its coloration. The Romans used carnelian to make stamps to imprint the wax seal on correspondence or other important documents, in fact hot wax does not stick to carnelian. Carnelian helps in understanding the inner self, strengthens and motivates concentration, helps in public speaking, increasing one's self-esteem. It is a stone of power and can bring success in one's life. Carnelian is used to counteract negative thoughts and doubts, and wearing this stone can prevent others from reading thoughts or influencing one's mind.

Carnelian is also mentioned in the Egyptian Book of the Dead, to be placed in tombs as "magic armor" for life after death. The ancient Egyptians associated it with the goddess Isis because of her red color. The goddess, finding the limbs of her beloved husband Osiris, killed by her brother Set, recomposed them of hers, bringing him back to life. From this legend Carnelian is thought to have the same vital and energetic properties as blood, instilling courage to face fears, including that of death. In the Renaissance, used in magic, carnelian was usually engraved with images of warriors, and used as a magical amulet as protection against spells.

Another famous amulet that uses carnelian is the Eye of Horus, which is believed to offer protection against the evil eye. Carnelian is often used for blood purification, facilitating its flow into tissues and organs so as to help the assimilation of vitamins.

- Among other properties it helps the elimination of toxins from the body, the stimulation of the small intestine and metabolism as well as the treatment of diarrhea and all intestinal problems in general, favoring digestion.
- Corniola is used to relieve pain in the kidneys, for the treatment of asthma and for problems of the abdomen and bladder; it is even used for the treatment of cystitis and prostate problems and the entire urinary tract.

Among other qualities we can include the ability to cure infertility, to facilitate the resolution of problems with the uterus, to strengthen the eyes, the gums and to make the skin younger and more elastic. During pregnancy it is advisable to place it on the belly because this brings serenity to the unborn child.

Corniola has a very slow but decisive action; for this reason it must be used in a very long time. Very strong elixirs are made from this stone, with all the different preparation methods.

Eye of the Tiger

The stone called "tiger's eye" is a quartz crystal, with beautiful golden yellow bands running through it. It is a powerful mineral that helps harmony and balance, improving states of anxiety and fear. It stimulates action and helps to make decisions with discernment and understanding, as well as with great mental clarity. Traditionally it is used as an amulet against negative energies, and is known to induce courage, self-confidence and willpower. It enhances creativity and is one of the stones that help awaken the Kundalini. Tiger's eye stone has a reputation as a wonderful gemstone for attracting material wealth (and for enhancing the stability needed to maintain such wealth), abundance, stimulating the growth of Kundalini energy and therefore personal vitality. However tiger eye also has powerful spiritual uses.

Most of these stones come from South Africa, but they are also found in Brazil, India, Burma, Australia and the United States. The meaning of the name "tiger eye" derives from the fact that it resembles the iris of the feline: the color ranges from yellow to brown and brown, crossed by beautiful streaked shades.

The mineral is a great energy amplifier, as is the case with most quartz crystals, and will in turn increase the energy of any other crystals it is used with.

The particular, almost liquid movement of the light reflecting through the stone itself has always made the tiger's eye an excellent tool for vision or for divination work. The stone combines the energy of the Earth with that of the Sun, keeping the rooting of the person who uses it strong, thus also revealing itself as an excellent meditation stone. It enhances courage and tenacity, allowing these attributes to always be balanced with mental clarity and a joyful outlook.

The properties of the tiger's eye are also used to be able to discern the truth in every situation and to help understand the life one is living. The benefits can help slow down the flow of energy through the body, which makes the gemstone very helpful for stress-related ailments.

- Excellent stone for arthritis and inflammation of bone tissue.
- It is said to be useful in cases of schizophrenia, various mental disorders and impulsive obsession.
- Promotes better energy flow through the body when worn.
- It thus becomes an excellent stone for concentration, especially for those with attention deficits.
- Tiger's Eye can be used to enhance psychic abilities and aid the activity of the third eye chakra.

It is suggested to use tiger's eye in combination with Hyaline Quartz, Serpentine and Moonstone.

The tiger eye also stimulates the increase of Kundalini energy, the coiled snake that resides at the base of the spine. When stimulated, it can ascend through the spine: this process is said to lead to enlightenment. If you want to use tiger eye for this purpose, you can combine serpentine with it, which in turn will facilitate the Kundalini awakening process.

Jade

Jade owes its term since the time of the Spanish conquest of Central America, where this stone was highly prized and finely worked, to the Spanish phrase "piedra de yjada" (coined in 1565) which means "stone of the loins", since it was believed to be very effective in healing lower back pain and kidney ailments. Jade is among the oldest objects found from antiquity dating back to about 7,000 years ago and given its hardness, it was used to produce weapons and ritual knives. The working of jade in China (called "yu") has continued uninterruptedly for 5,000 years to create finely crafted objects of worship, since jade, in Chinese tradition, symbolizes the five virtues of humanity:

- Wisdom.
- Compassion.
- Justice.
- Modesty.
- Courage.

Jade is especially helpful for those who react to changes in weather conditions, it greatly stabilizes and balances the masculine and feminine energy of the wearer.

- Jade is a stone that can help achieve our goals by instilling resourcefulness and allows us to see beyond our self-imposed limitations and manifest our ideas in the physical world.

- Jade stone is considered a stone that helps and propitiates economic luck.

It can be used to bring money into our lives. It helps us to create a positive attitude towards money and to use it creatively and productively. It helps in internal digestive disorders, strengthens the whole body, protects against fatigue and extends life span. The properties of jade (preferably together with amber and chalcopyrite) are very protective and particularly suitable for children against childhood diseases.

It is excellent if you want to experience more vivid dreams, while if you want to gain a greater understanding of psychic dreams, try sleeping with jade under your pillow or on your nightstand for some time.

Heliotrope

The term heliotrope comes from the Greek words helios, meaning the sun, and tropos, manner. This is because in ancient times heliotrope stones were said to be able to reflect the sun: it is probable that the appearance of the heliotrope resembled the setting sun with the reflections of red that stood out in the ocean. Christian worshipers during the Middle Ages often used heliotrope to carve crucifixion scenes of Christ and martyrs, leading to heliotrope also being nicknamed martyr stone.

Heliotrope has been used since ancient times to increase personal energy and physical strength. Instills calm, especially in survival situations, and increases adaptability and organizational power, decreasing confusion and anxiety.

It is often used to purify and detoxify the body, it purifies the lower chakras, realigning their energies. Heliotrope has always been used in ritual magic. In ancient Babylon, it was used in rituals against enemies and in ancient Egypt used to open space-time gates and break ties. Heliotrope can help enhance intuition and creativity, and can be used to combat fatigue and confusion. It is good to keep a heliotrope in any place where its energy needs to be very clean. Even today heliotrope is used as a medicine and aphrodisiac in India.

Selenite

Selenite owes its term to the Greek "selenites" literally "moonstone", from the name of the Greek goddess of the moon, Selene.

Not to be confused with the Moonstone, another of the most beautiful and luminescent precious stones.

Selenite contains a lot of feminine energy and is often used to connect and communicate with the Divine. In the past it was often used as a magic wand to facilitate the conveyance of one's intentions for the Higher Self or the Universe.

Selenite is the stone of tranquility, it gives a very high vibration, and is capable of instilling mental clarity and a deep sense of inner peace, providing flexibility to our nature and strength for our important decisions.

It is a stone that goes well with intense spiritual work, especially in meditation, as well as being a powerful crystal of psychic communication. It can aid in communication in the past tense with ancestors and spirit guides.

Selenite also has the wonderful property of being able to energetically purify and cleanse other crystals of heavy energies. It can help at the cellular level, the spine and the skeletal system, it is used to improve skin tone and the body's ability to absorb calcium.

Ancient popular beliefs, but common all over our planet, have also emphasized the use of selenite to increase libido.

The properties of selenite are often used in magic to evoke protection from the realm of the dead and to also dispel negative energy in environments. Excellent reveals itself in esotericism if used on special grids, or around the house or in the corners of a room (together with the salt, but without touching), to create a safe and peaceful space.

Aragonite

Aragonite owes its name to the place where it was discovered, i.e. in the province of Aragon in Spain. Aragonite is a good stone for family and companionship, it is also a popular gemstone for soothing inner restlessness and stress jitters, providing mental and emotional balance. The properties of aragonite direct energy towards self-discipline, helping to persevere despite the limitations that life often has before us. It helps us better understand that these limitations represent how we interact with the world and life, and often determine our spiritual and physical growth.

Aragonite has historically been used to banish the heat of fevers, reduce inflammation and calm the nervous system. Orange Aragonite is a good remedy for small or large emotional traumas, helping to unblock the energy nodes related to the thought processing cycle and consequently favors concentration.

Being an excellent energy balancer, Aragonite manages to stabilize the different changes of the soul during our life, following the various properties inherent in the different colors. Aragonite therefore helps to open a glimmer of altruism, generosity and understanding in relationships with each other. It also acts on the metabolism, in the case of the white or blue variety, balancing the nervous system so as to relieve tremors and involuntary movements.

The orange variety is an excellent aid for the immune system, promotes the proper functioning of the digestive system and gives strength to the bones, muscles and vertebrae.

With Aragonite you can prepare very bland elixirs with all methods of preparation by immersion in water or cooking.

Aventurine

Its name means "ventura" (by chance) deriving from a very similar glass discovered by chance, in fact, in the eighteenth century in the city of Venice. Aventurine has been used for several centuries in the making of jewellery, vases and other ornamental pieces. They were found in the Omo valley in Ethiopia, primitive tools of aventurine used as points and axes, dated about 2 million years. Aventurine stone has the ability to enhance its user's sense of humor and gaiety. It's also an excellent balancing stone, it gives inner balance and stimulates dreams. It has a positive effect on the psyche, reinforcing a sense of individualism, and is the ideal stone for those seeking a positive outlook on life. Aventurine is useful in ailments of the lungs, sinus and heart, and to help increase muscle flexibility.

It can help balance the innermost and dormant emotions (great combination with malachite) and is one of the best stones to wear or carry during times of stress. It is also historically known for being able to bring out the heat of fever and inflammation. If we use multiple aventurine stones in the bath water, they become soothing stones for emotional pain and fears.

Stone of the sun

The stone of the sun is also known by the name of heliolite, whose meaning derives from the Greek "helios" which means "sun" and from "lithos" which means "stone".

The sunstone was used in Ancient Greece to represent the Sun God, Helios (or Apollo). In Greece the sunstone was believed to invigorate and improve the state of the physical body and spirit, bringing renewed health to both.

This particular gemstone was prized by ancient wizards, who used the sunstone to attract the power of the sun by associating it with power and material wealth. Sunstone properties are known for its powerful connection to light and the power of the sun, imparting a sunny character. It brings light to all situations and is an optimal stone for the second chakra in particular and all chakras in general. It is a powerful stone to dispel fears and phobias of all kinds, it increases willpower, as well as personal vital energy.

It can provide the stamina and energy needed to undertake projects and activities that may encounter objective obstacles. Excellent for the chronicity of sore throats and to relieve the pain of gastric ulcers. Also used for cartilage, rheumatism and general pains. It also helps in finding and maintaining a successful sexual relationship.

Brought in close contact, it stimulates the personal power of attraction.

The properties of the stone of the sun are enhanced if used together with the moonstone, especially in solstices, in personal rituals, in energy works and spells. Together they represent the balance of power between physical characteristics and psychic and spiritual characteristics.

Sunstone is very useful in removing energy ties or karmic threads from other people or things, and proves to be a fundamental stone in crystal healing given the energy boost it can add to other stones.

www.ingramcontent.com/pod-product-compliance
Lightning Source LLC
Chambersburg PA
CBHW071259040426
42444CB00009B/1794